ALSO BY LES MURRAY

The Vernacular Republic: Selected Poems

The Daylight Moon and Other Poems

The Rabbiter's Bounty: Collected Poems

The Boys Who Stole the Funeral: A Novel Sequence

Dog Fox Field

Translations from the Natural World

Subhuman Redneck Poems

Fredy Neptune: A Novel in Verse

Learning Human: Selected Poems

Conscious and Verbal

Poems the Size of Photographs

The Biplane Houses

Taller When Prone

Killing the Black Dog

New Selected Poems

Waiting for the Past

Continuous Creation

Continuous Creation

Last Poems

LES MURRAY

FARRAR, STRAUS AND GIROUX

NEW YORK

Farrar, Straus and Giroux
120 Broadway, New York 10271

Originally published in 2022 by Black Inc., Australia
Published in the United States in 2022 by Farrar, Straus and Giroux
First American paperback edition, 2023

The Library of Congress has cataloged the hardcover edition as follows:
Names: Murray, Les A., 1938–2019, author.
Title: Continuous creation : last poems / Les Murray.
Description: New York : Farrar, Straus and Giroux, 2022.
Identifiers: LCCN 2021057039 | ISBN 9780374605636 (hardcover)
Subjects: LCGFT: Poetry.
Classification: LCC PR9619.3.M83 C68 2022 | DDC 821/.914—
    dc23/eng/20211129
LC record available at https://lccn.loc.gov/2021057039

Paperback ISBN: 978-0-374-60788-3

Designed by Marilyn de Castro

Our books may be purchased in bulk for promotional,
educational, or business use. Please contact your local bookseller
or the Macmillan Corporate and Premium Sales Department at
1-800-221-7945, extension 5442, or by email at
MacmillanSpecialMarkets@macmillan.com.

www.fsgbooks.com
www.twitter.com/fsgbooks • www.facebook.com/fsgbooks

P1

To the glory of God

CONTENTS

A Note on the Text

JAMIE GRANT

'I think I've got about three-quarters of a new book ready,' Les Murray told me and my wife, Margaret Connolly, who was Les's literary agent, on our last visit to the house in Bunyah where he had spent a large part of his life. It was November of 2018, and Les had only five more months to live.

In the years leading up to that day, his literary work had been confronted with a series of obstacles. His old typewriter had broken, and could not be repaired, while a second-hand replacement typewriter sent by a well-meaning friend did not work either. As Les continued to refuse to enter the digital world himself, he had come to rely on his wife, Valerie, to type out his new poems on the computer she had purchased. But Valerie, as a result of an unsuccessful knee replacement operation, was no longer able to walk to her study. Les, too, was almost completely immobile.

In October, he had resigned from his position as Literary Editor of *Quadrant* magazine after a tenure of more than thirty years. As we spoke with him, that day in November, it became apparent that his usual mental acuity was in decline, so we couldn't be sure whether or not that new book really existed.

At the end of April in the following year, his long journey came to an end. Then came the complications of probate, and arrangements for a State Memorial, while Valerie had to move into a nursing home. Before we could return to Bunyah, the Covid pandemic arrived, and no one in New South Wales was allowed to travel beyond their immediate neighbourhood. Not until October of 2020 did it become possible for us, accompanied by John Vaughan, the Murray family lawyer, to make our way along the gravel road that leads toward the humble wooden structure that once housed the author of the most distinguished body of work produced by any Australian poet.

The garden outside was overgrown and the living areas were chaotic, but the study where Les had written his poems seemed as if he had just left it – the bookshelves clean and well-organised, the desk tidy with writing pads and pens in place, the broken typewriter pushed to one side. In the centre of the desk lay a black spring-backed folder, and, just as Les had said, about three-quarters of a book's worth of poems were inside the folder, all typed out by Valerie. On the floor beside the desk was a large cardboard box, like one of the boxes seen in a removalist's van, filled to the brim with pieces of paper. The box contained all of the past five years or so of correspondence Les had received, along with multiple handwritten drafts of the finished poems that were in the folder, and further drafts of poems that had not yet been typed out.

There were multiple drafts of these untyped poems, too, and I decided to type out what seemed to me the latest and best versions of these drafts, relying entirely on what Les had written rather than trying to 'finish' or edit his words. The last seventeen poems in this collection (from 'Azolla' onward), as well as the poem 'Exile' – which seemed to me a companion piece to 'Balz's Fosterling', a poem that Les had published internationally in the preceding year – are the result, amounting to roughly a quarter of a book.

When Les was interviewed by *The Paris Review*, he claimed of his writing methods, 'I often don't have many drafts in handwriting,' but the contents of the box disproved this assertion. Instead, the box was proof of just how meticulous a craftsman Les had been, and of how hard he worked to polish every line, even of those poems that read like spontaneous quips.

Beside the box on the floor, under the desk, were the three massive volumes of the project Les referred to, again in his *Paris Review* interview, as his hobby: 'I collect images, postcards, photos, bits of verse, weird newspaper snippets, labels. They all go into big old-style ledger books to which Clare gave the title "The Great Book", pronounced in Scots.' (Clare is the younger of the two Murray daughters.) Each volume took a decade to compile, and in the latest one can be found the source material for some of the poems I have added to this collection. A somewhat mystifying poem called 'The Breast Depot' is clarified by a photo pasted into 'The Great Buik', while the reference to 'Clare's albums' in 'On Bushfire Warning Day' becomes self-explanatory.

These ledger books will, in due course, be deposited in a library, providing scholars and interested readers alike with indispensable insight into the mind behind the poetry. The collection of poems in the folder did not have a title, so I have chosen to name it after one of the briefest of them, a title which could be seen as summing up its author's life's work.

Continuous Creation

THE INLAND FOOD BOWL

A gapped circle of colonies
each staring at the ocean
through a glass plaid of imports.

Inland lies the still uncrowded
heartland once of steamboats and drawl,
now half desert, half freshwater province.

There the Murray descends its seven thousand
feet off the Pilot, zigzags over the plains,
forest and furrow, towards an outfall wash.

Shallow rivers connect to this one, or slant north
where the dragon Ceratodus grunts in ivory mail
and streets are shaded in peppercorn and willow.

Having monstered tribesfolk,
dressed POWs in maroon,
it now flickers dials, or pipes experienced water

onto rice, onto cotton, on to Adelaide,
Western rivers merge down the Darling
above the flint blade

and reburied bones of the Warrior
as snow wind chills the saltbush
down from seven thousand feet.

BOARDING IN TOWN FOR SCHOOL

The trick was to be
asleep before the rail signalman
whispered in with his latest
girl off the midnight train

otherwise the murmurings
would go on and on
whatever the pair did –
At waking they'd be gone.

Those days when boys called you
names that rarely impressed
the girls, who danced, calling you
like Hinder and Posterio;

those days could be got through,
spit on prefects, eat downtown,
talk cadet rifles,
admire one or two.

Staying with your best friend
at his place. And his sister
coming in in worn bathers,
knocking bedframe with her broom,

a year older than you,
quiet touch in her face,
city ahead, and your lies
to dismiss her so undue.

THE INVENTION OF PIGS

Come our one great bushfire
pigs, sty-released, declined to quit
their pavements of gravel and shit.
Other beasts ran headlong, whipping

off with genitals pinched high.
Human mothers taught their infants creek-dipping.
Fathers galloped, gale-blown blaze stripping
grass at their heels and on by

too swift to ignite any houses.
One horse baked in a tin shed,
naked poultry lay about dead
having been plucked in mid flight

but where pigs had been legion
only fuzzy white hoofprints crowded
upwind over black, B B B
and none stayed feral in our region.

TROPICAL HAND FOOD

Cassava, cassava
this lady of New Britain
told me it could be eaten,
the root and the jube,
the pithy stems and tube.
Cassava, mandioca,
green fruit of tapioca,
irradiate leaves and tremor,
wise lady of New Britain.

A FRIENDSHIP

i.m. Robert Ellis 1942–2016

Thrown out of another suburban house
in the Boarding age, I gloomily stood
reading the Vacancies pinned up in the Quad
Wanted: a roommate, alas must be male –
That had spirit, so we met in North Bondi's
Raffles Hotel, Lismore teenager and scrag
in a twelve-hour argument, Bible Adventist
vs apprentice Catholic, we hit it off well.

The Raffles was Dutch, KLM crew layoff,
the owner, widely feared in Sydney, was one
Abe Saffron, who kept us incorrupt
in the year we spent there at movies and pool.
When his manageress evicted us for grot
he, returning from Hollywood, cast her out
in turn, and sent men to invite us back
but we had moved on to Midnight Cowboy

(then yet to be filmed) (it's how we lived, Murray)
back from Jedda-land, and a culture called the Push
which wasn't a film, I dared to marry –
he declared this would destroy art in me.
A month later, the Cuba crisis, he and two friends

fled to the mountains, and came back not nuked,
all related years after in a wonderful film
called *The Nostradamus Kid*, spurned in Australia.

Long before, he'd scripted *The Life and Times
of King O'Malley*, who sold twenty years
of his soul to Parliament and Nation,
capital and rail line, then slumped in silence.
Newsfront followed, whose hero kept his soul:
masterpieces all three; his career followed on
through film and prose, as mine through rough metre
but we were friends for friendship, not rivalry.

We made an arch biopic for TV
with a mute's breakout speech, which the ABC lost,
we made kids' film *I Own the Racecourse*.
He married adorably well, and out-ventured
a Kiplingite friend on behalf of Bangladesh
while I moved quietly home to the bush.
He was loyal to tin roofs among hosts who were not
and brought me friends among the filmed and the shot

but now our barely political yarns
are finished, even in the Jewish café
down Bondi, where last summer saw us
praising our fathers and Bill O'Reilly.
You are gone. And I had dared think

it was like when my liver went to the brink –
low slung and wooden, you pass on your way
as I prefer all our years to one dressy day.

TESTING THE CHAINSAWS

Cross cut and long cut,
test splits and loud chaw,
dry blade with grit pouring,
blood heaped on the floor.
Up-angled many-severed
black toast-crusty ends
clamped in ring steel.
Crack-faced open lightnings
ham sliced parallel,
fragrant screamy chock burr,
pistol-gripped and urged well.

THE SCORES, 20TH CENTURY

1901
When we were all servants
fending off Madam's slurs
the white girl ditched her baby
and the black girl kept hers
and a boy on his pony
taught it all about spurs
and the flowers were all golden wattle.

1921
That weak word the Battlers
I saw from the train
families punch hoods from wheat bags
to keep out the rain:
Tom said a seller's market
made Australian girls vain
and for Tom the flowers were poppies.

1941
Ar there, Ginger Meggs:
was it Susso tea and suet
put those callipers on your legs?
If Sister Kenny could do it

you'd walk again like a trooper,
left-right and left-right
and the wreaths would be Singapore orchids.

1961

We came because here were no politics
said your in-laws. Sweet monotonous languor!
And a pill was a sexless bore at school
but one brought bassinets under control;
you were young and free for longer:
somehow this caused great anger
and its songs came by disc from America.

1981

You rose dressing up
and you praised putting down
especially the cultures
of TV and bush town
the white-booted chucker
and the wet-lipped seersucker
and the flowers were flung gladioli.

2001

Fashion ruled, while the old Queen still reigned.
Some flickers of nonsense remained,

one last war, and none of ours killed –
Cuisine grew less shamed and more skilled,
Entertainment grew more forms of media,
some dearer, some seedier
yet the flowers were Olympic gold roses.

REPORTS AND MANAGEMENTS

A man, errant, with a thirsty knife
wanders the market on a crowded noon,
not a slicer of long melons, not
a shaver of green cabbage heads. Alarm
begins to peak, outward from him and
police run in, unsheathing
not their tasers, but their handguns
firing, hoary sergeants firing,
girl constables firing. Screams
rise from the tumbled knife-bearer,
from aged women, and older
shot in the legs as the fallen man is,
so many shins darkly trickling. Why
did the Force not wield its tasers,
designed to cripple menace, not
execute it? Not TV, not the Third World
of instant execution, surely – ?
not by the knife man attacking the constables
first, on the third day, as media now report it.
This could be a long inquiry and questioning
unless a deflecting account blows up
beyond the hospital screens. Lacking
suppression, this story could whiten
years of wigs. But we prejudge nothing.

METAL BIRTH

Big man leaving a small car
turns over, lies across his seat
grips the steering wheel and throws
out a pair of trampling feet
which bend
sleekly to the asphalt. He then
dips his face from under
the dash, up into view,
grinning at the end of an eclipse
and writhes upright, balancing, complete.

THE SOLSTICE VOTE

In June, the Northern hemisphere
lies around in gardens,
crust of rotting gold.

Beetroot, garlic and watermelon
are sovereign for blood pressure,
it's said, though after April

melon tastes like floodwater
in my latitudes.
The British are having

a referendum this solstice
to stay half in Europe or half out –
late, late. Better

they'd stayed out in 1914
like Norway after Viking.
Splintered washboards of cold

are nailed across our sky.
Perfect day for Tasmanian
salmon, and Tasmanian malts.

POLO SOLVED

Marco Polo of Venice
he travelled to China
by his account, and listed
much that he saw there,

bridges, printed banknotes,
ships, Emperor Kublai
but missed the Great Wall,
then ruinous, and hot tea.

Some of his country
called him a braggart,
Marco Millions, for centuries
but if you are autistic

things that you've missed
seem not to exist,
and if ladies are hidden
who sees their bound feet?

Seems he came halfway
home with the right princess
on a known sailing junk
sailing on the right day.

STEAM BATH WORLD

North, towards Polaris
primates born near zero
soak in volcanic water
glass melting in their fur,
apes of Hokkaido

and red-faced humans tip
buckets on scorching rock
under hides or timber
and burst out, nude and limber,
rolling in birch-tree shock.

Iceland, Russia, Finland,
Turkic speakers and Indio
tie a rank culture-headband
round the Earth's high forehead.
Their trusty towel is snow

that arch Rome never took to.
Sweat's their archaic soap.

WINDFALL

Kangaroo sleeping
ahead on the road turns out
to be twigs and leaves.

FAILFORD CEMETERY

Richard Hardy of Failford Cemetery
retired to rest in nineteen thirteen.
He was two years old when Trafalgar was fought
and his father was ship's carpenter of HMS *Victory*.
His uncle was the flag captain who supported
a dying Nelson on the ship's quarterdeck:
'Kismet, Hardy.' If the Royal Navy allowed
a captain and a carpenter of such consanguinity
to serve in one vessel, then Kiss me! indeed.
Sixty years Mr Hardy pioneered around Nabiac
and his wife bore him eighteen offspring, feasibly
pre, early, mid and late Victorian.

CONTINUOUS CREATION

We bring nothing into this world
except our gradual ability
to create it, out of all that vanishes
and all that will outlast us.

BALZ'S FOSTERLING

Sliding into bed
as into a holster,
Balz, of Zurich,
considers the servant maid
whose baby is just born.

Most will call it his.

Rifle in the cabinet
schnapps on the bureau,
the infant's real sire
dismissed to go to England.

I watched her mother
not go back to Ulm.

So the little noble one
shall keep her name
with me. Be my favourite:
first overcoat every winter.

Berta the baby grows
into an expert draper
modiste and rifle shot

and only in his cups
does Balthasar at times
bayonet the furniture.

EXILE

Balz dead, and war over
emigration is the plan
though Berta abhors it.

Hearing of it, her true father
summons her man –
What profession are you in, sir?

Schweizer Brauch. Swiss custom,
and you? *Astrology –
I shun this murder-continent.*

She will never forgive me
but take this money. It may help.
Why Australia? *I've long*

*corresponded with Bondi
Surf Lifesaving Club –*
They arrive on Melbourne Cup day

and are kept on board.
The money buys a block
and the footings of a cottage,

flooring where there's walking,
water hose piped through a window –
the children recite Grimm.

Years later, in comfort,
Berta chuckles, when told:
He bought me decent exile –

STUART DEVLIN'S SCULPTURE

Modern coins the sizes of shine
swept off my friend's bureau in Ghent
and pocketed by my careless habit –
not brown pennies too dull to return

they include designer Devlin's sculpture
of the duckbilled animal
swimming up to the top swirl
and five kangaroo tails mixed to a dollar.

When the Irish attained their republic
they mounted their noble beasts trim
each well inside a knurled rim
and labelled in lapidary Gaelic

while our successors simply enact
themselves: the lyrebird under music,
echidna belly-on like a buckle
each numerally off-centre and whacked.

What is the use of small change?
To pay small debts, toss up, delight children,
to gamble by the jingle-crash billion –
to clean your teeth, with the card tasting strange.

TRIMMING PLUMBAGO

With musical gasps
the cane knife comes
shaving the swollen
skirts of the hedgerow
and the falling stalk tips
cover ground with shallow
masses of sky blue
while the old-shaped
blade acquires a white edge
fresh and narrow as cotton
retouched with the stone

BINGHAM'S GHOST

Bingham, alias Lord Lucan
vanished for forty years
without a sign or a token
till his title devolved on his son.

Our earlier, flannel-shirt Bingham
vanished from company and speech
just round the time his workmate
turned solemn, with a new tale about him.

Bingham – his forenames didn't last –
had quit bush slog to go scan
for fresh graft down the Hunter Valley.
It had come time to abandon

the cheerless tramp after cedar
logs to fell and float down
the wintry floodwater gullies.
No place for follow-my-leader

but Bingham proved not wholly missing.
Odd times, in moleskins and coat
he'd appear by the Forestry roadside,
moveless, with his pockets pulled out

and patriarchs and other locals
shivered grimly at encounters with him.
Long gone now, he froze many a rider
and silenced whole carloads of revellers.

SILO PORTRAITS,
WESTERN VICTORIA

Way back were bullocks
and drapers and bankers
and women revved fabric
through sewing machines
for Dulcie and Lachlan
as silos bleached upward
shed-topped, cement high

but now cars don't stop
at the pubs. On to Brim,
on to Coonalpyn
since it's mainly locals
who now scorch into town
past sleepout and church
where teens return seldom

grinning up at gigantic
forerunners and themselves,
Tone, Maya and Guido
either side the dead railway,
faded, dust-purple
and lank as red hair.

HALF-PRICE HARDBACK

As the bookshops die
in country towns
it's department stores
that stock reader shelves

with detective fiction
with bisex romance
with veterans and war
with cookery and garden

and heaped gifts for children.
This is the culture:
no history but the Allied,
nothing strange. No poetry.

All's preserved slow TV
selling no local memoirs,
no spirit, no religion,
no theory, little foreign

except tourist guides,
no languages at all
only ever middlebrow,
the culture of habitual

SPEED

We only realise
how huge is the giraffe
when it is in towering flight
from the blackbeard lion
herding it towards its mate

and we see the lioness
erupt out of cover
to be shed, stomped,
rolled like a motor bike
under an express train.

We only realise how tough
the lioness is, limping off
unshattered as the mighty
galloper speeds on over
the desert horizon.

FREDERICK ARNALL

Son of a fugitive
alderman from Cornwall
my grandfather Fred
took up the shovel
in his early teens
to extract khaki alunite

from an upside-down mine
tunnelled inside a mountain
and send it cascading
down into commerce
as alum, the medicine that
fixed colours in cloth.

Marrying, he moved south
to dig refractive coal,
tarry fossil rock that still
powers half our world
and wrecks lung tissue. Did his,
dead at fifty. Wish we'd met.

Irony of coal, how it
synthesised Nature's hues.
Irony of his tallness

that left him and me
ancestrally Spanish

by the DNA I'd had
checked out in racial times,
not Koori as half hoped
but sherry Castellano
job-hunted long ago
across the Biscayne sea.

SCHOOL BUS HOME

Little kids and bigger kids
get trizzed up by their mother
and ride the mountain bus each day
chucking boredom at each other.

Poddy Foster goes to Gloucester
for his education.
He's learned to write and learned to fight
in the smell of menstruation.

Where he and his seniors used to quaff
the roadside's liquor orders
now he's sent to ride the bus each way
and the mail protects booze hoarders.

A rare word comes from Germany:
how is that tall sweet girl?
They mean you, Tanya. They met you –
eyes down, she smiles a growl

and the bus sets down parallel
with the fused lilli-pilli-shaded
course of the Wang Wauk River
webbing east to salt and the sea.

CHERRY SOLDIERS

Chokecherry, chokecherry, makin a stand:
I got your little pokeberry eatin from my hand.

THE CARS THAT SQUEEZED ME

Having won a heavy case
Driving in a Manner Dangerous
to the Public – which can mean jail –
I plumed myself for a week

till a letter came demanding
a thousand dollars in Court Costs,
rather more than I'd have lost –
Where now was the kind scarlet Beak?

'So, eh?' I murmured to the witness
who had secured my win,
as there swapped the Arresting Sergeant
between cars I'd never seen him in.

SWALLOWS RETURNING

Manoeuvre and zip
make a trio of two
swallows just returning
from winterless New Guinea

and now fetching clay
to plaster a cradle
under verandah beams
and nipping the odd spider –

swallows, now tremulous,
now whipping over glass.

GREEN CATBIRD

Freckle-headed green
catbird mews its territory
out of mid rainforest.

Both sexes may bound
up from branch to branch
heading for the canopy.

Catbird stays in the bush
paired or single, ready
to play the cripple

tapering off thereafter
into fruit and leaf meals,
telling their green storey.

PIPPIES

Knotted underwater
through ripple, looking out
until they twist upright
like darkening knife-handles
hardening, keenly split.

AUSTRALIAN PELICAN

Stately effortful bird
runs behind its lift
into takeoff and ascent,

rising out of millennia
with its rigged pink sail
climbing to migration.

Silent collective birds
immersing in unison
drain wrigglings of fish.

Gradually all over
the estuary, pelicans
share themselves singly
post by wharf by boat.

WEEBILL

Caught a weebill in my car grille,
bird twice the weight of a hefty beetle.
Only heard it when I left the bush.
If it couldn't home it would likely perish.

Extracted, it whirred off, copse and hollow.
I couldn't drive after it, couldn't follow
its speed among parrots and bigger birds.
I braked, and said a line of words.

All wasted. Its cohort would supply
its brood with forage, if it should die.
If not, it would announce its own homecoming
Relearning how to slow and sing.

1917 NORTH

Recruits who brought
their horses from home
left us to ride them

now we're on track
creaky saddle, supple back,
to find our way to Beersheba

with a tinny black pan
and a plate of scran
but only dribs of water,

up from Suez
leaving bakers and brewers.
Johnny's waiting in Beersheba.

Tomorrow's to be Gallipoli,
second time, for you and me
on horseback two years later.

We'll gallop through the town
heads or tails or penny brown
as we charge through Beersheba.

GALWAY EFFIGY

Polished shoulders
continue round the bowl
to support the neck

and the upright face
surprised yet sardonic
in its shaven skin.

The diminished arms
narrow in and vanish
under coloured sleeves

and there are no legs
in the cluttered dish.
Only the limp grey

hair above maintains
overshadowed vision
and signs of smart disease.

LAZE CREATES ISLAND

Lava, erupting as mass
stone on the boil, riding on scarlet.

Lava, capping. Absorbing roadbed.
Angular crash into homes.

Last views, loading.
Viewers still arriving.

Smoke pouring into sea off farms
cool surf, sinking glitter down

coarse dragons from above,
laze glass raining as ocean-clink.

VERTICALS

Whizz of blue striped
curtains on a rail
and beyond those, the dull
downrights of sheet iron
wrapped around fruit trees
to fence off horse-rubbing,
donkey-scrape, and the horns
which used to grind sugar.

AZOLLA

Moist red of green,
flat green of russet
spread over the swamps,
blanket of stillness
injured softly by ducks
by heron-legs, deep –

Azolla. Earth squash
arising as islets,
mandarin and orange
rolled and mud-sucked
or floating beyond,
beak-dug by crows.

Afternoon silver
under lilli-pilli trees
and the calmed water
fails to lift yet
but quivers overall
with minute skin-heavals.

Next dawn, the tissue
of water gapes wide
in opened leads,

transparent black
mirroring for miles,
clotted around trunks.

WAITING FOR THE PAST

Waiting for the past
you were unrehearsed
and the moment passed

flesh tells what mind forgets
you turn your mind to it
waiting for the past

the tortured never trust
never trust again
waiting for the past

all the strappy wars
you aren't forgiven for
return your mind to it

waiting for the past
and the receding star
burns through flesh afresh

CHEROKEE ROSE

A towering willow tree
refreshed by spring, and jammed
with soft white pearl-shell

a cascade of faces
down tiers and staircases
becoming a shatter

a darkening currency
distilled into a surface
spreading along lake water.

Berets and gob caps
increase above sailormen,
whole companies of headgear,

Cherokee from ancient China,
white, in unshaven Spanish,
buttony, mid-centre gold

but decaying thickly
into a second week
of ashy soda.

PARENTAL JOB SWAP

Sitting next to his flagon
on the morning stairs,
his wife on the bus
lovingly escaping eight children.

He hiccups the courage to go
to his emptied duties
and stay drunk enough to hold on
there while assuring dismissal –

he remembers that his wife
has finally taken her own job
and the bus, continually promoted,
dark jacket to silk-cream jacket,

rumbles like his gut in the day.
He, falling over his flagon
has suffered the good disaster
as his wife is promoted yet again

through the roof, above the children
who had been shielding him
as he dreams unpaid FM
world music; eee limo limo

her bus has been promoted
to two teenagers driving him
in her limo to his shrink
in hiccups, to drain his flagon.

THE ESTUARY WALK

Lightning up above the rain
knocks out the television
channel after channel, every spill
of lurid lego colour, till
only a golf match in Hawaii
and its burnished cup remain coherent –

I turn it off, and tread
boards and long carpet to bed,
hoist up the top sheet under quilt
so that if my bared feet escape
they'll flinch me back to an S-shape
coiled in the Genghis-yurt I've built.

After some nonexistence
I emerge on estuarine distance
that I have somehow fled into
and am compelled to cross, stepping
on buoying crates, running and dipping
as these kick and bound on panes of water

whatever follows quickly fades, ashore
but the skidding boxes stay in memory
as a fast dance on a crumbling paddlewheel,
like an episode from way back when I still

had my rollrock spryness, my agility.
Is that gone forever? Or retrievable?

after night purlers when there's no horizon,
for me, a comeback's not believable,
but not every letter on the dream shelf
is addressed to oneself –
so I lurch down two steps on a grab-bar

and as I do every day
retrieve my balance in the car
and drive off to hospital to see
one with a needle's eye design
on each long life line,
my dear one with her third right knee.

LIGHTNING STRIKE BY PHONE

Storm coming now. I must hang up –
she said, and was painfully slapped.
Indeed if the junction box outside
hadn't blown apart, she would have died

of the lightning that fused condensers
and blew them all over the paddock
and as her face burned and rang
a ball of lightning formed out along

the verandah, came snorting and strumming
to the door, and sucked inside
straight into the video, which came on
and displayed all it knew, its numbers,

all its jittering pathetic ruined numbers
that would never sing again, or tell a story.
A black cloud imprinted round the phone
marked it, too, as instant archaeology.

BELOW THE PADDOCK

Climbing up from the bywash
on boxed timber stairs

lengthens the lucid dam
kinking back
lethargically

choosing cards to play
among bent lotus stems.

ON BUSHFIRE WARNING DAY

What would we take?
fridge stuff, money cards,
clothing, Clare's albums,
my Jenny Compton sweater.

Where would the cat go?
Bush. Where would we go?
Newcastle, at best,
or else as roads were open.

Would we come back?
If the house survived, yes,
even if all remaining were
tiles and fuselage metal.

Erasure might be
a sort of rebirthing,
a new tune, higher strung,
new ceilings for new clouds –

If we stayed gone
we'd be pestilent lore,
present in our past
crowding the new people.

ALL BLACKS IN THE
SAME HOTEL

They hang together
in this nest of chairs,
they barely answer

in the lift, on stairs.
Could be my accent –
must be the most suspect,

closest, known to all;
am I offering shares?
They slope off to practice,

Thames-ward daily, behind
worn blue palings,
remote nation, defined

by sea and play, both vast,
by thigh-slap, gruff wailings,
and they'll leave here last.

A JUNCTURE

Frosty-eyed Ben Boyd, sailing
back from California without gold
has vanished in the Solomons –
eaten, his crewmen guess
fingering their Sam Colt pistols.

In Port Macquarie, they learn
that gold has been found in Australia –
fossickers overrun the last chained men.

Who'll free our captain's
blackbirds? They was freeing themselves
when we sailed –
I'm for the diggings, me.

They watch the Wanderer's fittings
sway off, sand-deep on a cart –
Do they Christless blackamoors eat men?
Like ours don't?

BREAK OF AUTUMN

Crepe myrtles from China
branch-heavy with mauve and rain,
black waterfowl moving ghostly
in grass to the scarlet of their brows
belladonna, belladonna.
The cat reaches under its chin
and switches on its brisk engine.

NAP

Stretched out on the sofa,
it is forty years ago
old friends young as
each other. As me.
Entangled in courtship
of long-forgotten girls
everyone is more British,
dressier, pre-Twiggy in woollens
and desert boots, but
with a touch of *traktor*
though in bungalow suburbs.
A girl is ferrying me
in her car, but stops to
lay plans. Detailed and sensible
in incessant prose
as John Cleese on TV
breaks through. I prefer the girl
but Cleese is dulcet, ringed
by awed interviewers. We age,
white haired, as he has turned
several of us have died.
Many never saw this studio.

HUSBANDRY

You cannot drink bread
you can't butter beer
and it takes at least two men
to plough with a spear –
yet here we are
yet we've got here.

HAPPY FAMILY BIRDS

Common babbler, fussy, Happy Jack the jumper,
chatterer, codlin-moth devourer, dog bird
the twenty-named, yahoo, the dormitarian,
parson bird, pine bird, twelve-apostle bird

working the ground, turnover of leaf litter,
probers of soil, uppers of under-branch-chips,
pale to red breasted, catbird, big-nest heaper,
four metre up, thin billed, buff sided.

Wee-oo, at play together, flash-tail striper
co-op breeder in gangs of a dozen, mum
with predators around, noisy at grass play,
fledglings squeal begging, *wee-ink* while resting.

THE BREAST DEPOT

Seeing dumpy soil
ascend an incline with grey-blue
plastic triangles scattered up it
it's hard not to think skirmish,
new graves on a battlefield –

but our son, maybe noticing
the drumsticks at the corners
holding the plastics open
around shadowy infant trees
cries *I knew it: the mammofarm.*

DATELINE

Like old-time washerwomen
floodwater is sousing trees and shrubs
down in the gully. Floating wrack
dribbles seaward from their labour.

Last time rain poured day and night
like this, it was refilling the land
after months of desert.
The deluge spreads mirror over roads.

Human effort gets its pages turned
and the media display towns
blanked under windribby parchment.
We are hearing Tornado and Tsunami

at home, words unknown in teapot times.
Downpour and Inferno are states
that people drive between
pensioning their senators and whitegoods.

Global warming's chiller winters
rule both hemispheres. Arizona snow golf,
Siberian wheat, English vineyards
stricken by blizzard in their chardonnay.

Sportsfolk misusing pharmacy face
ruin. Arts folk taking drugs boast of it.
Slapped mud makes Saharan cities cool
but this week HIV spared an infant.

Asteroids sped above the fried milk of Canton
but this very week HIV quit an infant.

THE MYSTERY

A black hearse of Howards
undertakers of Taree
leads a long procession
toward Krambach's paddock cemetery.

As it passes Purfleet,
the aboriginal mission, old Mr
Lobban, Uncle Eddie
last initiated man
of the Kattang, stands beside
the then gravel road, with hat
doffed, as no one ever sees it.

Many mourners of the dead
woman will long remember,
name names and speculate.
Lobban, Worth, Syron –
names likely to signal
intermarriage mostly live east of Bunyah
but are subtly scattered,
not always known, even to women.

The boy the dead woman
has commanded be well schooled
crouches under the grief

that has wrecked his father's dignity.
He resolves never to cry.

Years till he will fathom
the blame that screams between
his parent and grandfather.
It is understood, not named.
His father is disinherited
for a brother's death.

Years till the boy grasps
that the older man will accept no land
ever, except on Bunyah.

ACKNOWLEDGEMENTS

Poems in this collection have been published in the *Australian Poetry Journal, Fiddlehead, Image, The Monthly, PN Review, Poetry Chicago, Quadrant, Rialto* and *The Spectator*. An earlier version of 'The Scores' was published in *Poems the Size of Photographs*, and later reprinted in *Collected Poems*.

CPSIA information can be obtained
at www.ICGtesting.com
Printed in the USA
LVHW040559120623
749491LV00002B/398